Publishers Disclaimer
Whilst every effort has been made to ensure that the information contained is correct, the publisher cannot be held responsible for any errors and or omissions. Please note certain recipes may contain nuts or nut oil.

First published in 2013. © Like Books & Design Ltd 2013
PRINTED IN CHINA

Whether creating a tasty snack, a hearty soup or stew, a succulent roast, a super quick stir fry or even a batch of homemade cookies, nothing beats the smell of delicious home cooking filling your kitchen. This journal allows you to keep track of all your favourite recipes - whether they are your own tried and tested favourites, a recipe from a favourite restaurant, or a recipe lovingly passed down through your family and friends - there is plenty of space to include the recipes in the sections within the journal, or in the storage pocket at the back of the book.

Included are more than 60 easy to follow step-by-step recipes to help you on your way to creating your own definitive recipe collection, which can be referred to time and again.

In cookery there are many terms used in recipes for different cooking or mixing methods, and if you are not familiar with these terms a recipe can seem daunting, so here are some of the main terms you may come across and an explanation of what they mean.

Al dente   A term used to describe the correct texture when cooking pasta and vegetables. The food should have a slight resistance when biting into it.

Bake   To cook in an oven.

Baste   To spoon, brush, or squirt a liquid (meat juices, stock, melted oils or fats) on food while it cooks to prevent drying out and to add flavour.

Beat   To mix ingredients together using a fast, circular movement with a spoon, fork, whisk or mixer.

Blend   To mix ingredients together gently with a spoon, fork, or until combined.

Boil   To cook until liquid is so hot it forms bubbles.

Braise	To cook where meat or vegetables are first browned in butter and/or oil, then cooked in a covered pot in a small amount of cooking liquid at low heat for a long period of time. This cooking process both tenderises the food by breaking down their fibers and creates a full flavoured dish.
Broil	To cook directly under a heating element.
Brown	To cook over medium or high heat until surface of food browns or darkens.
Bouquet garni	A small bundle of herbs, tied together or placed together in a piece of muslin or cheesecloth, used to enhance the flavour of a soup or stew. The classic combination of herbs is parsley, thyme, and bay leaf.
Chill	To place in the refrigerator to lower a food's temperature.
Chop	To cut into pieces with a sharp knife or chopper.
Combine	To mix ingredients together.
Cream	To beat until smooth, soft and fluffy.
Cube	To cut into 1/4inch cubes.
Cut	To mix a solid fat into a flour mixture with a pastry blender, a fork or two knives
Dice	To cut food into 1/8inch cubes.
Dot	Drop bits of butter or cheese here and there over food.
Drain	To pour off liquid.
Dredge	To lightly coat food to be pan fried or sauteed typically with flour, cornmeal, or breadcrumbs.

Flour	To coat greased pans or dishes with a fine coat of flour. Shake out extra flour.
Fold	To mix gently by bringing rubber scraper down through mixture, across the bottom, up and over top until blended.
Fry	To cook in hot fat.
Garnish	To decorate a finished dish with colorful food to make it look pretty.
Grate	Rub against a grater to cut into small shreds.
Grease	To spread the bottom and/or sides of a pan with shortening to prevent sticking.
Grill	To cook directly over a heating element or hot coals.
Knead	To fold, turn, and press dough with heel of your hand in order to develop the gluten and make dough more elastic.
Ladle	To dip and serve liquid with a ladle.
Marinate	To soak food in a liquid to tenderise or add flavour to it (the liquid is called a marinade).
Melt	To heat until it liquefies.
Mince	To chop or cut into tiny pieces.
Mix	To stir foods together.
Panfry	To cook in fat in a skillet.
Parboil	To partially cook food in boiling water before completely cooking by some other process.

Pare	To cut off the outside skin, as from an apple or potato.
Peel	To pull off the outer skin, as from a banana or an orange.
Pit	To take out the seeds.
Poach	To cook a food by partially or completely submerging it in a simmering liquid.
Preheat	To turn oven on ahead of time so that it is at the desired temperature when needed (about 5 to 10 minutes).
Puree	To mash food until it has a thick, smooth consistency usually done by a blender or food processor.
Roll	Flatten and spread with a rolling pin.
Rubbing in	Rubbing pieces of cold diced butter or fat into flour using the fingertips and lifting the flour at the same time to avoid clumping.
Saute	To cook in small amount of fat in a skillet/frying pan.
Scald	To heat milk just below a boiling point. Tiny bubbles will form around the edge.
Score	To make shallow cuts into the surface of foods such as fish, meat, or chicken breasts to aid in the absorption of a marinade, to help tenderise, and/or to decorate.
Sear	To brown a food, usually meat, quickly on all sides using a high heat to seal in the juices.
Shred	To cut into very thin strips.

Shortening	Modern shortening is a vegetable-based product, such as Crisco®, that is just barely solid at room temperature. Shortening has a higher smoke point than butter and margarine, leading to its use in deep-fat frying and as a pan coating to prevent baked goods from sticking.
Sift	To put dry ingredients like flour through a sifter or sieve.
Simmer	To cook in liquid over low heat so bubbles form slowly.
Steam	To cook food over steam without putting the food directly in water (easier when done with a steamer).
Stir	To mix round and round with a spoon.
Stir Fry	To quickly cook small pieces of food over high heat while constantly stirring the food until it is crisply tender (usually done in a wok).
Sweat	To cook slowly over low heat in butter, usually covered, without browning.
Toss	To mix lightly.
Well	A hole made in dry ingredients in which you pour liquid.
Whip	To beat with a rotary egg beater or electric mixer to add air.

soups & starters

Cream of Asparagus Soup

(Serves 4)

Rich, velvety, & full of flavour.

1 ltr chicken or vegetable stock
450g/1lb fresh asparagus, trimmed
olive oil
2 small potatoes, peeled and roughly chopped
2 onions, peeled and roughly chopped
50ml/2 fl oz double cream or creme fraiche

Method

Prepare the asparagus by discarding any old and woody pieces from the bottom of the stalk. Using a sharp knife remove the tender green spears from the top of the asparagus. Bring a small pan of salted water to the boil and cook the spears for 1 minute only, drain, and plunge into a bowl of iced water, this will retain the beautiful green colour, these will be used to garnish the soup later. Roughly chop the remainder of the stalks.

In a large pan fry the chopped onions in 1 tbsp of olive oil until slightly soft but not coloured, add the chopped potatoes, asparagus and stock, bring to the boil. Reduce the heat and simmer gently for about 20 minutes or until the potatoes and asparagus stalks are soft and tender.

Transfer the soup to a food processor or using a hand held blender, blend the soup until smooth and silky. Return the soup to the pan and add the drained asparagus spears and stir in the cream and warm through. Season to taste with salt and freshly ground white pepper. Spoon into warmed serving bowls and serve with crusty bread.

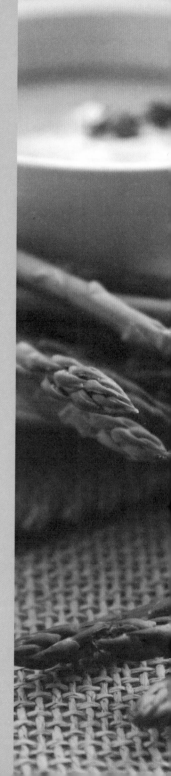

French Onion Soup (Serves 4)

A classic soup, hearty, warming and satisfying. Soft, sticky caramelised onions simmered in beef stock enhanced with a dash of brandy, topped with a crisp crouton and melted bubbling Gruyere cheese, simply delicious.

50g/2oz butter
1kg/2.2lb onions, peeled and thinly sliced
2 tbsps thyme leaves
3 tbsps brandy
1.2 litres good beef stock

For the croutons

1 small French baguette, sliced on the diagonal
1 garlic clove, peeled
olive oil
110g/4oz grated Gruyere cheese

Method

Heat the butter in a large heavy based saucepan, add the onions and thyme and cook the onions until soft but not coloured for about 20 minutes, increase the heat slightly and cook for another 10-15 minutes until the onions become dark, golden, sticky and caramelised, stirring occasionally.

Add the brandy, cook for a further 2-3 minutes burning off the alcohol, add the beef stock, bring to the boil, reduce the heat, then simmer for 20 minutes. Season with salt if required and a good twist of freshly ground black pepper.

Meanwhile preheat the grill to high. Toast the French stick slices until golden brown, then rub each slice with the garlic clove. Transfer the hot soup to warmed serving bowls and place on a baking sheet. Top each soup bowl with the crouton, top generously with the grated Gruyere cheese and place the bowls under the hot grill until the cheese topped croutons are golden and bubbling. Carefully remove the bowls from the grill and serve immediately.

Roasted Garlic, Tomato & Basil Soup

(Serves 2)

Simply delicious, a taste of the Mediterranean, this recipe is great for the summer months if you have a glut of tomatoes to use up.

1kg/2.2lb ripe tomatoes
1 ltr chicken or vegetable stock
2 red onions, peeled and cut into quarters
4 garlic cloves, unpeeled
1/2 bunch fresh basil
olive oil
balsamic vinegar
salt and pepper

Method

Preheat the oven to 180C/350F/Gas mark 4. Cut the tomatoes in half, and then place them on a baking sheet together with the onions and garlic cloves. Roasting garlic in their skins stops the garlic from burning, the cloves will become beautifully sweet when roasted which will add a truly wonderful flavour to the finished soup. Drizzle liberally with olive oil, a generous seasoning of salt and freshly ground black pepper and a good splash of balsamic vinegar.

Place the tray in the oven for 30-40 minutes or until the tomatoes are slightly charred and the skins have blistered and the onions have softened. Remove from the oven, and then transfer the tomatoes and onions with all the beautiful flavoured oil and vinegar into a food processor. Squeeze the garlic cloves from their skins and add to the tomatoes.

Carefully add the boiling stock to the tomatoes in the blender, add the basil and blend until the soup is smooth. Season the soup to taste with salt and freshly ground black pepper if requires. Serve the soup in warmed bowls garnished with fresh basil leaves and a drizzle of good olive oil.

Stilton & Celery Soup (Serves 4)

The perfect winter warmer, simply delicious.

25g/1oz butter
1 onion, peeled roughly chopped
5 sticks celery, roughly chopped
110g/4oz potatoes, peeled, cut into small pieces
280ml/10 fl oz full fat milk
280ml/10 fl oz chicken or vegetable stock
75g/2 1/2oz stilton cheese, crumbled
50ml/2 fl oz single cream
chopped parsley to serve

Method

Melt the butter in a large saucepan, add the chopped onions and celery and fry for 5 minutes, stirring occasionally until soft but not coloured. Add the chopped potatoes, then add the milk and stock and simmer for 20 minutes or until the potatoes are tender.

Liquidise the soup until smooth and return to the pan, if the soup is too thick, simply add a touch more milk or stock to bring to the desired consistency. Season to taste with salt and freshly ground black pepper. Gently reheat the soup, then add the crumbled stilton cheese, stir through until melted. Pour into warmed serving bowls and top with a swirl of cream and the chopped fresh parsley.

Watercress Soup (Serves 4-6)

Deliciously fresh flavoured soup packed full of nutrients.

250g/9oz fresh watercress
1 onion, peeled, finely chopped
1 garlic clove, peeled, crushed
olive oil
50g/2oz butter
500ml/18 fl oz chicken stock
225g/8oz potatoes, peeled, thinly sliced
400ml/14 fl oz milk
110ml/4 oz single cream
few leaves of fresh watercress to garnish

Method

Heat the butter and a drizzle of oil in a large pan and sweat the onions for 2-3 minutes until soft but not coloured. Add the garlic and fry for a further minute or two. Add the potatoes and stock, season with salt and white pepper, cover with a lid and simmer for 10 minutes or until to the potatoes are tender. Add the watercress and continue to simmer for a further 2 minutes. Do not cook the watercress too long as you want to retain the bright vibrant colour.

Transfer the soup to a food processor or using a hand held blender, blend the soup until smooth. Adjust the seasoning if necessary. Return the soup to the pan and add all but 2 tablespoons of the cream and gently stir and warm through.

Pour the soup into warmed bowls, drizzle over the remaining cream and garnish with a few leaves of fresh watercress and serve with crusty bread.

Mushroom & Gruyère Soufflé (Serves 8)

Delicious and surprisingly easy to make!

150g/5oz button mushrooms, sliced
50g/2oz butter, plus extra for greasing
25g/1oz flour
325ml/11 fl oz milk
3 large eggs, separated
110g/4oz Gruyere cheese, grated, plus a little extra to serve
6 tbsps creme fraiche
pinch of cayenne pepper
mixed salad leaves to serve

Method

In a medium sized pan, melt the butter over a moderate heat, then fry the mushrooms for 2-3 minutes until just soft. Remove a third of the mushrooms from the pan and set aside. Add the flour to the pan with the remainder of the mushrooms and the butter and stir well until the flour is blended in with the butter. Gradually add the milk, stirring all the time until the sauce is thickened and is smooth and silky.

Season with salt and freshly ground black pepper and a touch of cayenne pepper. Stir in the grated cheese until melted, remove from the heat and set aside. Heat the oven to 200C/400F/Gas mark 6. Butter 8 x 150ml individual ramekins or souffle dishes and place a small disc of greaseproof paper in the base of each dish. Stir the egg yolks into the cheese sauce, then take a separate bowl and whisk the egg whites until firm. Take a third of the beaten egg whites and mix into the cheese sauce to loosen the mixture slightly, then carefully but thoroughly, fold the remaining whites into the sauce until the mixture is well combined, light and fluffy.

Spoon the souffle mixture into the prepared dishes, run your thumb around the rim of the dish to clean the edge. Half fill a roasting tin with hot water. Place the dishes in the water bath then bake for 12-15 minutes until well risen and golden brown.

Remove from the oven, take the dishes out of the water then leave to cool. They will sink, but don't worry, they are meant to. Cover and chill until ready to serve. Turn the souffles out of their dishes, then peel off the disc of paper from the bottom.

Place the souffles on a baking sheet lined with parchment paper. Top each souffle with 1 tsp of creme fraiche, the reserved mushrooms and a sprinkling of grated Gruyere cheese. Bake in a preheated oven at 190C/375F/Gas mark 5 for 10-12 minutes until slightly risen and warmed through. Remove from the oven, transfer to serving plates, place a small handful of mixed dressed salad leaves on the side of the plate and serve immediately.

Melba Toast with Potted Shrimp (Serves 4)

This dish has a lovely old-fashioned feel to it and making potted shrimp is as easy as they are delicious.

4 slices bread, 1cm thick
250g/9oz peeled brown shrimp
100g/3 1/2oz unsalted butter
pinch cayenne pepper
pinch ground allspice
fresh ground black pepper

Method

Preheat the oven to 180C/350F/Gas mark 4. Toast the bread on both sides, then cut off the crusts and cut the slices into triangles. Use a serrated knife to split each piece of bread down the middle into two slices. Place on a baking sheet and bake for about 5 minutes until dry, crisp, and slightly curled. Meanwhile, melt the butter over a very low heat (it should be just warm enough to melt, not cook). Add the shrimp and the spices, stir, then divide among 4 small ramekins. Take to the table with the toast.

Smoked Salmon & Horseradish Blinis

(Makes 24)

Smoked salmon with a hint of lemon zest, served on a blini, topped with a horseradish cream.

1 lemon, juice and zest
200g/7oz smoked salmon, finely chopped into small dice
24 ready made blinis
1 shallot, peeled, finely chopped
142ml/5 fl oz soured cream
2 tsps creamed horseradish sauce
small bunch of fresh dill, finely chopped
freshly ground black pepper

Method

Place the chopped smoked salmon into a bowl, add the juice of half the lemon and a good seasoning of freshly ground black pepper. Stir in the finely chopped shallot and the lemon zest. Combine the soured cream with the horseradish sauce. Spread the cream mixture onto the base of the blinis, then top with the chopped smoked salmon. Top each blini with some finely chopped fresh dill and serve.

Smoked Haddock Pâté with Cayenne Pitta Crisps (Serves 4)

1 x 250g/9oz undyed smoked haddock fillet
1 unwaxed lemon, zest finely grated, plus 2 tbsp juice
100g/3 1/2oz soft cheese
1 x 15g pack fresh chives, finely chopped
2 tbsps capers in brine, drained, rinsed and chopped
For the pitta crisps
2 white pittas
2 tsps olive oil
pinch cayenne pepper

Method

Preheat the oven to 180C/350F/Gas mark 4. Place the fish in a medium-sized shallow pan, cover with cold water, then bring to the boil over a high heat. Put a lid on the pan, remove from the heat and leave for 5 minutes. Transfer the fish to a plate to cool. Pat the cooked fish with kitchen paper to dry. Remove any skin or bones and flake the flesh into the bowl of a food processor. Add the lemon zest, juice and soft cheese, then blend to make a coarse pate. Add the chopped chives and capers, and whizz briefly. Transfer to a bowl, cover, then chill for at least 2 hours.

Carefully cut each pitta through the middle. Place cut-side up on a chopping board and rub with a little olive oil then sprinkle with cayenne pepper. Cut each piece into rough triangles. Place on a baking sheet and cook in the oven for 5-6 minutes until golden brown. Serve with the pitta crisps.

Paprika Spiced Crab Pâté (Serves 8)

450g/1lb fresh white and dark crab meat
200ml/7 fl oz creme fraiche
2 tbsps mayonnaise
2 salad onions, finely chopped
1 tsp smoked paprika
1 x 15g pack fresh chives, chopped, reserving several blades to garnish
grated zest of 1 lemon
1 tbsp lemon juice
dash of Tabasco® sauce

Method

In a large bowl, mix together the mayonnaise, salad onions, paprika, chopped chives, lemon zest and juice, and Tabasco®. Season and gently fold in the crab meat. Gently fold the creme fraiche into the crab mixture. Divide the mixture between 8 ramekins, then cover and chill in the fridge for 30 minutes. Take the pate out of the fridge 20 minutes before serving. Garnish with the chive blades and serve with slices of melba toast (see page 16) and a wedge of lemon.

Wasabi Prawns (Serves 4)

King prawns, marinated in lime and ginger served with a hot and spicy wasabi mayonnaise.

20 large mediterranean, cooked and peeled
2 limes, zest only
1 red chilli, finely chopped
For the mayonnaise
110g/4oz good quality mayonnaise
2-3 tsps wasabi paste
little gem lettuce leaves
2 spring onions, trimmed, finely sliced
1-2 tbsps japanese rice wine
1 lime, zest and juice

Method

Mix the king prawns with the lime zest and chilli in a bowl, mix thoroughly together, then leave to marinate in the fridge for one hour. Meanwhile spoon the mayonnaise into a bowl, add the wasabi paste, spring onions, rice wine and lime juice and zest and mix together until well combined. Arrange the prawns in the lettuce leaves, then spoon over the mayonnaise and serve.

Goats Cheese & Parma Ham Figs (Serves 6)

3 ripe black figs
150g/5oz soft goats cheese,
150g/5oz Parma ham

Method

Cut the stalks off each of the figs and cut them into quarters. Top the cut side of each fig with a teaspoon of the cheese. Wrap with a slice of the Parma ham. Then spear each fig with a cocktail stick to secure and place on a large serving plate. Heat a frying pan and fry the wrapped figs for 3-4 minutes, turning halfway through, until the ham is crisp and the cheese is warm and melting.

My recipes

Recipe ....

Serves ....

Preparation time ....

Notes/tips ....

....

....

....

Ingredients

....

....

....

....

....

....

....

Method

My recipes

Recipe ....

Serves ....

Preparation time ....

Notes/tips ....

....

....

....

Ingredients

....

....

....

....

....

....

....

Method

My recipes

Recipe

Serves

Preparation time

Notes/tips

Ingredients

Method

My recipes

Recipe ....

Serves ....

Preparation time ....

Notes/tips ....

....

....

....

Ingredients

....

....

....

....

....

....

....

Method

My recipes

Recipe ....

Serves ....

Preparation time ....

Notes/tips ....

....

....

....

Ingredients

....

....

....

....

....

....

....

Method

My recipes

Recipe ....

Serves ....

Preparation time ....

Notes/tips ....

....

....

....

Ingredients

....

....

....

....

....

....

....

....

Method

My recipes

Recipe ....

Serves ....

Preparation time ....

Notes/tips ....

....

....

....

Ingredients

....

....

....

....

....

....

....

Method

fish & seafood

Thai Fish Cakes (Serves 8)

Delicately spiced fish cakes, so simple to prepare, served with a sweet and sour dipping sauce. The fish cakes can be made before hand, just leaving you to finish them off as your friends arrive, a little last minute work, but well worth the effort, they are simply delicious.

450g/1lb cod, haddock or coley fillets, skinned, cut into chunks
1 tbsp thai fish sauce
1 tbsp thai red curry paste
1 tsp palm sugar or muscovado sugar
1 kafiir lime leaf or 1 strip of lime zest, finely shredded
1 tbsp chopped fresh coriander
1 egg
1/2 tsp salt
50g/2oz french beans, sliced thinly into rounds
150ml/5 fl oz groundnut or sunflower oil
For the Sweet & Sour Dipping Sauce
50ml/2 fl oz white wine vinegar
110g/4oz caster sugar
1 1/2 tbsp water
2 tsps thai fish sauce
50g/2oz cucumber, diced very finely
25g/1oz carrot, peeled, diced very finely
25g/1oz onion, peeled. chopped very finely
2 red chillies, sliced thinly

Method

To make the sauce, gently heat the vinegar, sugar and water in a small pan until the sugar has dissolved, bring to the boil for 1 minute, then leave to cool. Stir in the fish sauce, cucumber, carrot, onion and chillies, pour into a serving bowl and set aside.

For the fish cakes, place the fish in a food processor with the fish sauce, curry paste, lime leaf or lemon zest, chopped coriander, egg, sugar and salt, then blitz until smooth. Stir in the finely chopped green beans. (Do not put the green beans in the food processor, as you want them to retain the shape and create a different texture in the fish cakes).

Divide the mixture into 16 pieces. Roll each one into a ball, then flatten slightly into a 2 1/2 inch disc. Heat the oil in a large frying pan, then fry the fish cakes in batches for a minute on either side, until golden brown. Lift out and drain on kitchen paper to remove any excess oil. Arrange the fish cakes on a large serving plate and serve with the dipping sauce.

Tandoori Spiced Salmon

(Serves 4)

A simple dish to prepare, soft, moist pieces of salmon, mildly spiced with ginger and garlic. This dish can easily be prepared before hand and left in the marinade until you are ready to serve, just bake in the oven for 10 minutes and serve.

4 x 175g/6oz salmon fillet portions or steaks
6 tbsps natural yoghurt
1 tsp garam masala
1 tsp paprika
small piece fresh ginger, peeled and grated
1/2 tsp ground cumin
2 garlic cloves, peeled and crushed
lime wedges to serve

Method

Place the marinade ingredients together in a large bowl, season well with salt and freshly ground black pepper and mix thoroughly until all the ingredients are well combined.

Place the salmon pieces in the marinade and ensure they are coated completely in the spiced marinade, turning occasionally. Cover the bowl, then set aside in the fridge until you are ready to serve.

Preheat the oven to 200C/400F/Gas Mark 6. Remove the salmon from the marinade and place onto a lightly greased baking tray, place in the preheated oven for about 10 minutes or until the fish is just cooked through. Remove from the oven and serve immediately with lime wedges to spritz over the top.

Healthy Fish & Chips (Serves 2)

A light, healthy and simply delicious oven baked fish and chips recipe served with a tangy refreshing homemade tartare sauce. You can substitute the potatoes for sweet potatoes if you wish, I also love to add a pinch of chilli flakes to the potatoes to give them a spicy kick.

450g/1lb potatoes,washed, skin left on, cut into chips
1 tbsp olive oil
1 lemon, juice and grated zest
2 white fish fillets, use your favourite, each weighing about 150g/5oz
1 tbsp capers
4 small gherkins, finely chopped
2 tbsps 0% fat greek yoghurt
chopped fresh parsley
lemon wedge to serve

Method

Preheat the oven to 180C/350F/Gas mark 4. Toss the unpeeled chips in the olive oil and season with salt and freshly ground black pepper. Place the chips onto a baking sheet in an even layer for about 30 minutes or until the chips are golden brown and crisp on the outside and soft on the inside. Half way through cooking the chips, give the tray a little shake and turn the chips over so they cook evenly.

Place the fish fillets into a shallow dish, brush the fillets lightly with oil, season with salt and pepper and drizzle over half the lemon juice. Place in the oven along with the chips and bake for 12-15 minutes. After 10 minutes, sprinkle over the lemon zest and a little chopped parsley to finish cooking.

Meanwhile as the fish and chips are cooking, mix together the yoghurt, capers, gherkins, remaining parsley and lemon juice, season with salt if required and freshly ground black pepper and mix thoroughly to combine all the ingredients. Remove the fish and chips from the oven and transfer to two warmed plates and serve with the tartare sauce and a lemon wedge.

Smoked Trout & Warm Jersey Royals

(Serves 2)

450g/1lb jersey royal potatoes
small bunch of tarragon, chopped
1/2 red onion, peeled and finely chopped
2 tbsps olive oil
1 tbsp red wine vinegar
6 spring onions, finely sliced
50g/2oz rocket leaves
175g/6oz smoked trout
salt and black pepper

Method

Cook the potatoes in boiling salted water for about 10 minutes until just
tender, drain and when cool enough to handle cut into thick slices. Mix
together the tarragon, red onion, vinegar and oil to make the dressing, season
with salt and freshly ground black pepper.

Pour 3/4 of the dressing over the warm potatoes and mix. Add the spring
onions and rocket, then gently mix again. Divide between 2 serving plates and
top with the smoked trout, finish with the remaining dressing.

Soy Glazed Tuna Steaks (Serves 4)

Spice up your tuna - simple and healthy.

4 fresh tuna steaks, each weighing about 150g/5oz each
50ml/2 fl oz soy sauce
2 tbsps clear honey
1 garlic clove, peeled, crushed
1 tsp sesame oil

Method

Mix the Soy sauce, sesame oil, honey and garlic in a bowl until well combined. Place the tuna steaks in a shallow dish, then cover with the marinade, cover with clingfilm, place in the fridge and leave to marinate for 1 hour, turning halfway through.

Heat a non stick pan over a medium high heat and fry the tuna for one minute on either side for rare, 2 minutes for medium, basting constantly with the marinade, until sticky on the outside. Serve immediately.

Optional: Serve with some steamed Chinese Bok Choi leaves, drizzled with lime juice, olive oil and sprinkled with toasted sesame seeds.

Thai Poached Salmon (Serves 2)

Transform a piece of salmon into a lovely fragrant meal, in no time at all.

1 tbsp of thai red or green curry paste
2 x salmon fillet portions (about 6-8oz/175-225g each)
200ml/7 fl oz carton of coconut cream
a handful of fresh coriander leaves, chopped
olive oil

Method

Add a drizzle of oil into a medium frying pan, add the curry paste and cook over a moderate heat for 30 seconds or so just to release all the fragrant spices. Add the coconut cream and bring to a simmer. Add the salmon fillets, cover, then simmer gently for about 7-8 minutes, turning the fish over halfway through.

Serve the salmon with some plain boiled rice and a generous sprinkling of freshly chopped coriander on top. This dish is delicious served with some freshly steamed fine green beans.

Prawn Linguine (Serves 4)

300g/10 1/2 oz raw peeled prawns
400g/14oz dried linguine
500g/1lb 2oz vine-ripened cherry tomatoes, halved
2 tbsps olive oil
3 garlic cloves, finely chopped
4 tsps fresh basil leaves, chopped

Method

Preheat the oven to 200C/400F/Gas mark 6. Spread the tomatoes over the base of a small roasting tin to fit tightly. Drizzle with 1 tablespoon olive oil and season. Roast for 25 minutes. Meanwhile, run a small, sharp knife along the back of each prawn to just cut through the flesh. Pull away any small black veins that you find.

Bring a large pan of lightly salted water to the boil. Add the pasta and cook until al dente. Just before the pasta is ready, heat the remaining oil in a large frying pan. Add the garlic, sizzle for a few seconds, then add the prawns. Toss them together over high heat for 2 minutes, until they are cooked through.

Drain the pasta, return it to the pan and add the roasted tomatoes, prawns, basil and some seasoning. Toss together well, divide between warmed pasta bowls and serve, scattered with a few small basil leaves.

Grilled Sardines (Serves 4)

8 x fresh sardines, cleaned and gutted
For the marinade
1 shallot, finely chopped
2 tbsps olive oil
2 garlic cloves, crushed
juice and rind of 1 lemon
juice and rind of 1 lime
1 tsp brown sugar
1 tsp balsamic vinegar
1 tbsp poppy seeds

Method

To prepare the marinade, simply combine all the ingredients together until thoroughly mixed. Place the sardines in a shallow dish and pour the marinade over, leave to stand for at least 20 minutes, but up to an hour if you have the time.

Remove the sardines from the marinade, place on a tray, under a preheated grill for about 8-10 minutes, turning once, until the fish is cooked through. This recipe can also be used for mackerel, try cooking the sardines on a BBQ, they will have a lovely charred flavour.

Fish Pie (Serves 6)

300g/10 1/2oz smoked haddock fillet, pin bones removed
300g/10 1/2oz haddock fillet, pin bones removed
300g/10 1/2oz salmon fillet, pin bones removed
1 onion, peeled, sliced
750ml/1 1/4 pints milk
75ml/3 fl oz white wine
110g/4oz frozen peas
3 hard boiled eggs, cut into quarters
3 tbsps freshly chopped parsley
50g/2oz plain flour
50g/2oz butter
salt and pepper
For the topping
1kg/2.2lb potatoes, peeled, cut into equal sized pieces
110g/4oz butter
75g/2 1/2oz grated cheddar cheese
splash of cream

Method

Preheat the oven to 200C/400F/Gas mark 6. Place the milk and onions in a large shallow saucepan and bring up to the boil, then reduce the heat to a very gentle simmer. Add the smoked haddock, haddock and salmon and cook very gently for 4-5 minutes.

Remove the fish carefully with a slotted spoon and set aside to cool. Reserve the cooking milk for the sauce. Melt the butter in a saucepan, add the flour and stir well to make a roux, gradually stir in warm milk, stirring constantly to create a smooth sauce, stir in the wine and simmer for 2-3 minutes.

Season to taste with salt and freshly ground black pepper. Then set aside and keep warm. When the fish is cool enough to handle, remove the skin and flake the fillet into large bite sized pieces. Place the fish into a suitably sized ovenproof dish.

Meanwhile cook the potatoes in boiling salted water until tender, drain well, then mash until smooth, then beat in the butter and a splash of cream, season to taste with salt and black pepper. Place the peas, parsley and eggs into the dish and combine with the flaked fish, ensuring all the fish and eggs are evenly distributed in the dish. Pour the sauce over the fish and carefully mix together ensuring all the fish is evenly coated in the sauce.

Carefully spoon the mashed potatoes over the filling to cover it completely, sprinkle over the grated cheese and place in the preheated oven for 25-30 minutes or until the topping is beautifully golden brown and the filling is bubbling hot.

Baked Salmon & Pesto Crust (Serves 4)

4 salmon fillet portions
1 jar pesto
50g/2oz parmesan cheese
1 lemon

Method

Place the salmon fillets on a baking tray, coat each fillet with the pesto, sprinkle over the grated cheese and a good squeeze of fresh lemon juice. Place in a moderate oven for 12-15 minutes until the fish is just cooked and the pesto and cheese have formed a golden brown crust on top. Delicious served with pasta.

Grilled Masala Mackerel (Serves 2)

A simply delicious healthy spicy supper dish - try and use only the freshest fish.

2 large whole mackerel
1 jar curry masala paste
1 lemon

Method

Make 4 or 5 incisions with a sharp knife along each side of the mackerel and rub the masala paste into the cuts. Place onto a baking sheet and place under a preheated moderate grill for approx 8-9 minutes turning the fish over halfway through. Remove from the grill and squeeze a generous amount of lemon juice over each fish. Serve with some crisp green salad leaves and a simple tomato salad.

Baked Sea Bass (Serves 2)

1 whole sea bass (cleaned, scaled and gutted)
1 bunch fresh basil
1 lemon thinly sliced
1 red onion finely sliced
splash of dry white wine

Method

Preheat oven to 180C/350F/Gas mark 4. Place the whole fish on a large sheet of baking paper. This method of cooking is known as En papillote. The food is put into a folded pouch or parcel and then baked. The parcel is typically made from folded baking paper, but foil may be used.

Using a sharp knife, make 4-5 incisions on either side of the fish. Open the cavity of the fish and place inside, half of the sliced onions, half the basil leaves, a few slices of lemon and season generously with salt and freshly ground black pepper. The parcel holds in moisture to steam the food but add just a splash of white wine (or water if you prefer) to ensure the fish does not dry out.

Place the remainder of the herbs, lemon and onions under and on top of the fish ensuring some of the basil leaves are pushed firmly inside the cuts on the fish. Drizzle generous amounts of olive oil on top of the fish and gather up the sides of the baking paper and either tie with string, or fix with a paperclip at each end (if you have any) creating a secure parcel. If you are using paper clips, remember they will be extremely hot when removed from the oven. Do not wrap the parcel too tightly as you want to allow the fish to bake/steam inside the bag

Place the fish on a baking sheet and bake in the preheated oven for 25 minutes. Take the unopened parcel to the table and savour the aromas as you open it, simply delicious.

My recipes

Recipe ....

Serves ....

Preparation time ....

Notes/tips ....

....

....

....

Ingredients

....

....

....

....

....

....

....

....

Method

My recipes

Recipe ....

Serves ....

Preparation time ....

Notes/tips ....

....

....

....

Ingredients

....

....

....

....

....

....

....

....

Method

My recipes

Recipe ....

Serves ....

Preparation time ....

Notes/tips ....

....

....

....

Ingredients

....

....

....

....

....

....

....

....

Method

My recipes

Recipe ....

Serves ....

Preparation time ....

Notes/tips ....

....

....

....

Ingredients

....

....

....

....

....

....

....

Method

My recipes

Recipe

Serves

Preparation time

Notes/tips

Ingredients

Method

My recipes

Recipe ....

Serves ....

Preparation time ....

Notes/tips ....

....

....

....

Ingredients

....

....

....

....

....

....

....

....

Method

My recipes

Recipe _____

Serves _____

Preparation time _____

Notes/tips _____

_____

_____

_____

Ingredients

Method

meat & poultry

Rustic Lamb Stew (Serves 6)

1.5kg/3lb 5oz of stewing lamb (cubed)
1 x 410g tin of chopped tomatoes
2 tbsps plain flour
2 cloves of garlic (crushed)
4 tbsps olive oil
175ml/6 fl oz of dry white wine
150ml/5 fl oz of lamb stock
1 sprig of fresh rosemary
1/2 tsp salt
salt & black pepper (to season)

Method

Cook at a high temperature. Place the flour in
a bowl and season with some black pepper.
Toss the lamb in the flour, coating each piece
well. Heat the oil in a pan and add the lamb.
Cook for 4-5 minutes, until lightly browned.
Transfer to the slow cooker.

Add the garlic to the pan and cook for
1 minute, followed by the lamb stock and
white wine. Bring to the boil, stirring
continuously. Pour over the lamb in the slow
cooker. Stir in the tomatoes and season with
salt and black pepper. Add a sprig of fresh
rosemary, cover and cook for about 1 & 1/2
hours.

Reduce the heat to low and continue to cook
for 6 to 8 hours, until the lamb is tender. Serve
with warm crusty bread.

Spicy Roast Lamb with Olive Oil Mash

(Serves 6)

1 part boned whole leg of lamb
2 cloves garlic, cut into slivers
For the marinade
4 tsps harissa paste
juice of 1/2 lemon
3 tbsps fresh mint, finely chopped
1 tbsp olive oil
For the mash
900g/2lb floury potatoes e.g. King Edward, peeled and diced
200ml/7 fl oz hot milk
3 tbsps extra virgin oil
For the roasted vegetables
1 red pepper, deseeded and diced
1 green pepper, deseeded and diced
1 yellow pepper, deseeded and diced
1 large aubergine, diced
2 tbsps olive oil

Method

Make several small incisions in the lamb and insert the slivers of garlic. Make the marinade, coat the lamb then cover and refrigerate for 4 hours or overnight. Place the lamb in a roasting tin in a preheated oven at 180C/350F/Gas mark 4 for 55-65 minutes per kg plus 25-30 minutes. About 35 minutes before the end of the cooking time toss the peppers and the aubergine in the olive oil, season to taste and cook for 40-45 minutes.

Place the potatoes in a pan of lightly salted boiling water, cover and simmer for 20 minutes, or until tender. Drain and mash until smooth with the hot milk and season. Beat in the olive oil. Keep warm until required. Remove the lamb from the oven, cover loosely with foil and allow to stand for 10 minutes before carving. Serve with the roasted vegetables and olive oil mash.

Slow-Roast Belly of Pork (Serves 2)

500-600g/1lb 2oz - 1lb 5oz pork belly joint
1 small handful of fresh sage, stalks discarded
1 small handful of pack fresh rosemary, stalks discarded
3 cloves garlic, roughly chopped
grated zest and juice of 1 unwaxed lemon

Method

Preheat the oven to 220C/425F/Gas mark 7. Roughly chop the sage and rosemary then, using a pestle and mortar, grind with the garlic and lemon juice and zest and seasoning to make a thick paste.

Cut the string off the pork and unroll the meat so that it is flat. With a sharp knife, make incisions into the flesh before rubbing the paste into the incisions and over the flesh, taking care to avoid the skin. Transfer to a roasting tray and, ideally, sit it on a rack. Using a piece of kitchen paper, thoroughly dry the skin and season with a little salt – this is optional, but helps make crisper crackling.

Roast for 20 minutes then reduce the oven to 170C/325F/Gas mark 3 for a further 2 hours until the pork is thoroughly cooked and the juices run clear. Leave to rest for 5 minutes then cut into chunks, and serve with steamed purple-sprouting broccoli and apple sauce.

Beef Bourguignon (Serves 6)

A true French classic with the beef marinated a day before the dish is cooked to add a rich depth of flavour.

1.3kg/3lb chuck braising steak cut into 2 inch pieces
225g/8oz pancetta or smoked streaky bacon, cut into lardons
450g/1lb shallots, peeled
2 bottles Burgundy wine
1 large carrot, cut into large pieces

1 large onion, peeled, roughly chopped
2 celery sticks, roughly chopped
2 sprigs of fresh thyme
1 whole head of garlic, halved
4 bay leaves
50g/2oz butter
50g/2oz plain flour
4 tbsps olive oil
300ml/10 1/2 fl oz beef stock
350g/12oz small chestnut or button mushrooms
5 tbsps brandy

Method

Heat 1 tablespoon of the oil in a large pan. Add the chopped carrot, onion and celery and fry gently for 3-4 minutes, stirring occasionally. Pour in the wine and add the sprigs of thyme, garlic and two of the bay leaves.

Bring the wine to the boil, then reduce the heat and simmer for 15 minutes. Remove from the heat and allow to cool completely. Pour the wine mixture into a large non-metallic bowl and add the pieces of beef. Mix well together then cover with clingfilm and set aside in the fridge to marinate overnight.

Preheat the oven to 150C/300F/Gas mark 2. Strain the beef into a colander set over a bowl, reserving the marinade and set aside. Heat half the butter and one tablespoon of oil in a large flameproof casserole dish and fry the bacon for a couple of minutes or until lightly golden brown. Stir in the shallots and fry for another minute or two. Remove the onions and bacon and set aside.

Heat another tablespoon of oil to the pan and fry the pieces of beef in batches until golden brown on all sides. Make sure you pat dry the beef pieces with kitchen paper after it comes out of the marinade or it will not brown.

Return the meat, bacon and shallots to the casserole dish. Pour in 2 tbsps of the reserved marinade into the casserole dish and allow to bubble away, use a wooden spoon to scrape all the sticky bits from the base of the pot. Sprinkle the flour into the pot, stirring and then add the remaining marinade, bay leaves and the stock, stirring well to combine all the ingredients.

Season with salt and freshly ground black pepper then bring to the boil, cover with a lid and place in the preheated oven for 3 hours or until the beef is meltingly tender but still holding its shape.

Halfway through cooking, heat the remaining butter in a large frying pan and cook the mushrooms for 3-4 minutes or until lightly golden brown. Pour in the brandy and burn off the alcohol. Transfer the mushrooms to the casserole dish for the remaining cooking time. When the beef is ready, season to taste, stir in the chopped parsley and serve straight to the table with crusty bread to hand around or a large bowl of soft buttery mashed potatoes.

Roast Rib of Beef (Serves 6 - 8)

The outer parts of the rib joint will be well done, with a peppery crust, while nearer the bone it will be pink.

3-3.5kg/6.6-7.7lb rib of beef
salt and freshly ground black pepper
50g/2oz butter, softened
1 pack fresh thyme
2 tsps green peppercorns, coarsely crushed
1 tbsp plain flour
1 large onion, thickly sliced
2 x 250g/9oz packs shallots, peeled but left whole
For the gravy
2 tbsps plain flour
500ml/18 fl oz beer
300ml/10 1/2 fl oz beef stock
pinch of dark brown sugar
few drops of Worcestershire sauce

Method

Preheat the oven to 230C/450F/Gas mark 8. Wash and dry the beef. Beat the butter with 2 tsps of the chopped thyme, the peppercorns and seasoning. Spread this on all sides of the beef and sprinkle it with the flour. Cover and chill for 2-3 hours.

Place the onion in a layer in the centre of a roasting tin and add a few sprigs of the thyme. Place the beef on top. Roast, uncovered, for 20 minutes, then lower the heat to 190C/375F/Gas mark 5. Cover the joint with foil and roast for 15 minutes per 450g/1lb, plus an extra 15-25 minutes if you prefer your beef medium to well done.

Roast the shallots, sprinkled with a little extra thyme, alongside the beef for the last 35-45 minutes of cooking. Remove the beef from the oven, transfer to a serving dish and tent with foil to keep warm for 20-30 minutes while you make the gravy.

For the gravy, place the roasting tin on the hob and spoon out any excess fat, leaving 3-4 tbsps in the tin. Stir in the flour, followed by the beer and beef stock. Simmer, stirring all the time, until thick and dark. Strain the liquid into a clean pan, and simmer gently for 10-15 minutes. Season, add the brown sugar and Worcestershire sauce, and stir in the juices from the carving tray.

Beef Wellington (Serves 6)

A classic, a stunning dinner party dish to impress your guests.

1.2kg/2lb 10oz fillet of beef
175g/6oz liver pate smooth
375g/13oz puff pastry
225g/8oz button mushrooms sliced

Method

Preheat the oven to 220C/425F/Gas mark 7. Heat 1 tablespoon of oil in a large frying pan. Season the beef with salt and pepper, and fry over a high heat until the meat is browned on all sides. Remove the beef and set aside.

Add the sliced button mushrooms to the pan and fry gently until just cooked, leave to cool slightly. Combine the pate with the mushrooms to form a paste. Roll out the puff pastry into a large rectangle (large enough to wrap around the beef) reserving any trimmings for decoration.

Spread the pate and mushroom mixture onto the puff pastry and place the beef on top. Roll the pastry over the meat to form a neat parcel, sealing the edges well using beaten egg. Decorate the top with any pastry trimming and place on a greased baking sheet.

Bake in the pre-heated oven, allowing 30-35 minutes for medium rare and 40-45 minutes for medium well done. Remove from the oven and allow to rest for 10 minutes before serving.

Turkey, Brie & Cranberry Burgers

(Serves 4)

500g/1lb 2oz, turkey mince
50g/2oz Brie, cubed
50g/2oz dried cranberries, roughly chopped
1 red onion, very finely chopped
2 slices white bread, crusts removed, torn up
1 tbsp tomato ketchup
1 garlic clove, crushed
1 tsp chopped fresh rosemary

Method

Soak the bread in a splash of milk and leave to stand for 5 minutes. Place the turkey mince in a large bowl, add the crushed garlic, finely chopped onion, rosemary, ketchup, dried cranberries and cubes of brie.

Squeeze out the excess milk from the soaked bread and add the softened bread to the bowl. Season with salt and freshly ground black pepper and mix all the ingredients until well combined.

Shape the mixture into equal sized patties and chill in the fridge for half an hour. Heat a griddle pan over a medium high heat, lightly brush the burgers with olive oil and place on the heated griddle pan and cook for 4-5 minutes on either side until golden brown and cooked through. Serve in toasted buns with crisp lettuce leaves and sliced tomatoes.

Chicken & Chorizo Chilli (Serves 4)

A simple chicken recipe, packed full of flavour. This dish can easily be prepared beforehand and re-heated as required. This recipe uses chicken thighs which I believe are far tastier than the breast, you can of course use chicken breasts if you wish, however the thighs have so much more flavour and are far less expensive. Add or reduce the amount of chilli you use according to your preferred taste. Dried chilli flakes can be substituted with fresh chillies, scraping out the seeds will reduce the heat, leaving a more subtle gentle heat to the finished dish.

8 boneless, skinless chicken thighs
1 tbsp olive oil
2 red peppers, de-seeded, cut into large pieces
1 x 400g/14oz tin, red kidney beans, drained
1 x 400g/14oz tin, chopped tomatoes
110g/4oz chorizo, peeled cut into chunks
1 large onion, peeled, roughly chopped
1 tsp dried chilli flakes
1 tsp smoked paprika
1 tbsp tomato puree
1 tsp dried oregano
1 chicken stock cube
2 garlic cloves, peeled, crushed
sour cream to serve

Method

Preheat the oven to 180C/350F/Gas mark 4. Heat the oil in a large pan over a medium heat and fry the onions for 3-4 minutes or until beginning to soften. Add the garlic and chorizo and fry for a further 2-3 minutes, stirring occasionally, until the chorizo has released all its wonderful fragrant oil.

Stir in the peppers, chopped tomatoes and tomato puree. Fill the empty tin of tomatoes half full of hot water and add to the pan together with the chilli flakes, oregano, paprika and the crumbled stock cube.

Place the chicken pieces on top of the sauce, pushing them under the liquid. Season the sauce with salt and freshly ground black pepper. Bring the dish to a gentle simmer on the stove, then cover with a lid and place in the preheated oven for 45 minutes.

Add the drained kidney beans to the pot and continue cooking for a further 20 minutes. Remove from the oven and serve with garlic bread, a spoonful of soured cream and a crisp green salad.

Spanish Style Chicken (Serves 4-6)

4 chicken thighs & 4 chicken drumsticks (skin on)
12 new potatoes, cut into bite size chunks
1/2 chorizo ring (approximately 110g/4oz), cut into coin size pieces
75g/2 1/2oz pancetta
280g/10oz jar chargrilled peppers, including oil
110g/4oz pitted black olives, drained (optional)
1 x 400g tin chopped tomatoes
2 tsps paprika
1 tsp cayenne pepper
4 garlic cloves, peeled and quartered
1 large red onion, peeled and quartered
1 tbsp olive oil
freshly ground black pepper

Method

In a large roasting tin add all of the ingredients and mix thoroughly. The best way to do this is to get your hands dirty so to speak - roll up your sleeves and mix!

Cook on a low heat at 150C/300F/Gas mark 2 for about 2 hours. Check during cooking that the dish is not drying out. If this happens, add a splash of wine or chicken stock, mix again and continue cooking. Check that the chicken has cooked and then turn up the temperature to 200C/400F/Gas mark 6 for about 15 minutes to crisp up the ingredients. Remove from the oven and serve.

Duck Pancakes & Hoisin Sauce (Serves 4)

A real favourite, spiced duck pancakes in a rich hoisin sauce, served with crunchy spring onions and cucumber. So easy to prepare yet simply delicious. This is a great sharing dish, place the duck in the centre of the table and let your friends create their own pancake rolls.

4 duck breasts, about 175g/6oz each, skins removed
1/2 tsp Chinese five spice
freshly ground black pepper
2 tbsps sesame oil
100ml/3 1/2 fl oz hoisin sauce
8-10 Chinese pancakes, warmed
1/2 cucumber, halved, seeds removed, cut into fine strips
1 bunch spring onions, trimmed, cut into thin strips

Method

Cut the duck breasts into thin strips, and then toss in the Chinese five spice powder and pepper. Heat the oil in a wok or frying pan over a high heat, add the duck, fry for 3-4 minutes, until crisp and golden brown.

Add the hoisin sauce, cook for 1 more minute until all the duck is coated in the sauce (leave the skin on the duck if you prefer, I love the flavour of the crispy duck skin, but the choice is yours). Transfer the duck to a warmed serving dish, arrange the spring onions and cucumber in a bowl, unwrap the warmed pancakes and tuck in.

Partridge With Mushroom Bruschettas

(Serves 4)

2 x 280g/10oz partridge
2 tbsps extra virgin olive oil
10g/1/3 oz porcini mushrooms
50g/2oz butter
350g/12oz mixed mushrooms (chestnut, button, oyster), brushed and roughly sliced just before cooking
2 large shallots, peeled and finely chopped
2 cloves of garlic, finely chopped
110ml/4 fl oz double cream
1 lemon, juiced
25g/1oz flat-leaf parsley, finely chopped
4 slices sourdough bread

Method

With poultry shears or sturdy scissors, cut out the partridge backbones. Press firmly on the birds so that they lie flat. Wipe clean with good kitchen towel. Season with salt, pepper and olive oil. Soak the porcini in 150ml/5fl oz boiling water. Leave for 20 minutes then strain; keep the juice.

Heat the remaining oil and butter in a frying pan until sizzling. Add all the mushrooms and the juice; when they are turning brown, add the shallots and garlic. Saute for a few minutes more. Add the cream, half the lemon juice and most of the parsley and season. Allow to bubble for a minute.

Heat a heavy-bottomed pan until smoking hot then add the partridge. Cook for 8 - 10 minutes a side until just cooked and squeeze over the remaining lemon juice. Halve the birds. Toast the sourdough bread and drizzle with extra virgin olive oil. Spoon the mushrooms onto each toast, top with half a partridge, scatter with parsley and serve.

My recipes

Recipe ....

Serves ....

Preparation time ....

Notes/tips ....

....

....

....

Ingredients

....

....

....

....

....

....

....

....

Method

My recipes

Recipe ....

Serves ....

Preparation time ....

Notes/tips ....

....

....

....

Ingredients

....

....

....

....

....

....

....

....

Method

My recipes

Recipe ....

Serves ....

Preparation time ....

Notes/tips ....

....

....

....

Ingredients

....

....

....

....

....

....

....

....

Method

My recipes

Recipe — — — — — — — — — — — — — — — — —

Serves — — — — — — — — — — — — — — — — —

Preparation time — — — — — — — — — — — — — — — — —

Notes/tips — — — — — — — — — — — — — — — — —

— —

— —

— —

Ingredients

— — — — — — — — — — — — — — — — —

— —

— —

— —

— —

— —

— —

Method

My recipes

Recipe ---------------------------------

Serves ---------------------------------

Preparation time ---------------------------------

Notes/tips ---------------------------------

Ingredients

Method

My recipes

Recipe ....

Serves ....

Preparation time ....

Notes/tips

....

....

....

Ingredients

....

....

....

....

....

....

....

Method

My recipes

Recipe   ....

Serves   ....

Preparation time   ....

Notes/tips

....

....

....

Ingredients

....

....

....

....

....

....

....

Method

pasta & rice

Pasta Carbonara (Serves 4)

A classic sauce, rich and creamy ideal to serve with spaghetti or tagliatelle pasta.

250g/9oz pasta
175g/6oz pancetta, or smoked streaky bacon, finely diced
5 egg yolks
150ml/5 fl oz double cream
110g/4oz parmesan cheese, half grated, half as shavings
handful of chopped parsley (optional)
salt and pepper

Method

Heat 1 tbsp of olive oil in a frying pan, add the pancetta and fry until crisp. Set aside, keep warm. In a large bowl mix together the egg yolks, cream and grated parmesan. Season well with freshly ground black pepper.

Cook the pasta, following packet instructions, in boiling salted water until just tender. Drain thoroughly. Add the freshly drained pasta to the egg yolk mixture, then mix and add the fried pancetta. Toss together immediately. Season to taste with salt and freshly ground black pepper.

Transfer to a warmed serving bowl. Top with parmesan shavings and garnish with freshly chopped parsley.

Spaghetti with Chilli, Olive Oil & Garlic

(Serves 2)

225g/8oz spaghetti
1 red chilli, deseeded and finely chopped
4 tbsps good quality olive oil
2 cloves garlic, peeled and chopped
salt and black pepper

Method

Cook the pasta according to the instructions on the packet. In the meantime. heat the olive oil in a frying pan and, when hot, add the garlic, chilli and a twist of fresh black pepper.

Cook over a low heat for a couple of minutes to allow the garlic and chilli to infuse the oil. When the pasta is cooked, drain then return to the saucepan. Add the chilli oil. Mix well, then serve on warmed pasta plates.

Ragu Sauce (Makes 6 x 225g/8oz portions)

A delicious authentic rich slow cooked Bolognaise sauce.

450g/1lb minced beef
450g/1lb minced pork shoulder
6 tbsps olive oil
225g/8oz chicken livers, cleaned and trimmed, finely sliced
2 large onions, peeled, finely chopped
4 garlic cloves, peeled, crushed
150g/5oz pancetta or streaky bacon, finely chopped
2 x 400g/14oz tins, Italian chopped tomatoes
400g/14oz concentrated tomato puree
400ml/14 fl oz red wine
1/2 tsp grated nutmeg
25g/1oz fresh torn basil leaves
salt and freshly ground black pepper

Method

Preheat the oven to 140C/275F/Gas mark 1. Begin by frying the onions and garlic in 3 tablespoons of the oil in a large frying pan over a medium heat for about 5-7 minutes, stirring occasionally until the onions are soft and lightly golden brown.

Add the chopped pancetta or streaky bacon to the onions and garlic and continue cooking for another 5 minutes. Transfer the onions, garlic and pancetta to a large ovenproof casserole dish. Heat another tablespoon of oil in the frying pan, turn the heat up to high and add the minced beef, breaking it up with a wooden spoon. When the meat is well browned transfer it to the casserole dish.

Heat another tablespoon of oil to the frying pan and repeat the process with the minced pork and add to the casserole dish. Heat the remaining oil and quickly fry the chicken livers for 2-3 minutes and add to the casserole dish.

You have now finished with the frying pan. Place the casserole dish over the heat and give everything a really good stir together, add the chopped tomatoes, tomato puree, red wine and a good seasoning of salt and freshly ground black pepper and the nutmeg. Give everything a really good stir to combine all the ingredients.

Allow this to come up to a gentle simmer, stir in half the basil leaves, cover the casserole dish with a lid and transfer to the preheated oven. Cook for 4 hours, stirring and checking occasionally. You will end up with a deeply rich concentrated sauce with very little liquid left. Taste and check for seasoning and stir in the remaining fresh basil.

Either serve the sauce with freshly cooked pasta while still hot, or leave to cool completely, and then transfer to freezer bags in 225g/8oz servings. When defrosted and reheated, each portion will provide enough sauce for 225g/8oz pasta, which will serve 2 people.

Pappardelle alla Bolognese

(Serves 6-8)

Rich ragu sauce finished with double cream and served with Pappardelle pasta make this dish such a heart-warming supper.

Ragu sauce (see recipe on page 93)
400g/14oz dried Pappardelle pasta
150ml/5 fl oz double cream
grated fresh parmesan
2 tbsps chopped fresh parsley
25g/1oz butter

Method

Cook the pasta in a large pan of boiling salted water, according to the instructions on the pack, until just cooked but still retaining a little bite. Heat the ragu sauce and stir in the double cream until fully incorporated and heated through.

Drain the pasta and toss into the hot meat sauce, stir in the butter, chopped parsley and serve with freshly grated parmesan cheese.

Lasagne (Serves 4)

Ragu sauce (see recipe on page 93)
lasagne sheets, dried
700ml/1.2 pt full fat milk
1 onion, peeled and cut in half, studded with 2 cloves
1 bay leaf
50g/2oz butter
pinch of grated nutmeg
50g/2oz plain flour
175g/6oz mature cheddar cheese, grated
50g/2oz parmesan, grated to finish

Method

Preheat the oven to 200C/400F/Gas mark 6. In a small saucepan, warm the milk, onion and bay leaf, until almost boiling, remove from the heat and leave to infuse for 10 minutes, then remove the bay leaf and onion. Melt the butter in a medium sized pan over a medium heat until foaming, add the flour, then cook, stirring continually using a wooden spoon for 1-2 minutes until the flour and butter has formed a smooth paste. Gradually add the warm milk, adding a little at a time, stirring continually until all the milk has been absorbed and the sauce is smooth and thickened.

Simmer gently for 4-5 minutes stirring occasionally. Remove the pan from the heat, and then add the grated cheddar cheese. Season with salt and pepper and add a pinch of grated nutmeg. Stir until the cheese has melted.

To assemble the lasagne, take an ovenproof baking dish and pour an even layer (about half an inch thick) of the ragu sauce into the bottom of the dish. Take the dried lasagne sheets and place in an even layer on top of the sauce. You may have to break up some of the pasta sheets to make them fit. Pour a thin layer of the white sauce over the pasta sheets. Repeat the layering process three times finishing with the white sauce on top. Sprinkle the top of the white sauce with the freshly grated parmesan cheese and bake in the preheated oven for 25-30 minutes or until the top is beautifully golden brown and the sauce bubbling up around the sides. Remove from the oven and serve.

Wild Mushrooms Risotto

(Serves 6)

50g/2oz porcini mushrooms
75g/2 1/2oz pancetta
25g/1oz unsalted butter
1 tbsp olive oil
1 onion, finely chopped
1 clove garlic, peeled and finely chopped
500g/1lb 2oz risotto rice
150m/5 fl oz red wine
2.5 pints/1.5 litres hot chicken stock
small handful fresh flat-leaf parsley, chopped
75g/2 1/2oz parmesan, grated

Method

Soak the mushrooms in 300ml warm, previously boiled water for 20 minutes.
Strain through a sieve, reserving the liquid. Roughly chop the mushrooms and

the pancetta, reserving 4 slices. In a large pan,
melt the butter with the oil, then stir in the
onion, garlic and chopped pancetta and cook for
3-4 minutes. Add the mushrooms and cook for
2-3 minutes, then add the rice and cook for
2 minutes, stirring. Pour in the wine and cook
until the liquid is absorbed, then stir in the
mushroom liquid and cook until this has been
absorbed. Season with freshly ground black
pepper. Add the hot stock, 130ml/4 1/2 fl oz at
a time, stirring constantly, until most of the
liquid has been absorbed. Cook until the rice is
tender but firm to the bite. Preheat the grill to
high. Place the remaining pancetta slices under
the grill and cook for 4 minutes until crispy,
then break into large pieces and add to the
risotto. Stir the parsley and parmesan into the
risotto and serve in warm bowls.

Garden Pea & Broad Bean Risotto with Dolcelatte

(Serves 4)

1 tbsp olive oil
1 large onion, peeled and chopped
2 garlic cloves, chopped
2 fresh thyme sprigs, leaves chopped
400g/14 oz risotto rice
150ml/5 fl oz dry white wine
2 - 2.5 pints/1.2 ‑ 1.5 litres hot vegetable stock
250g/9oz garden peas
250g/9oz broad beans, peeled
150g/5oz dolcelatte, roughly diced

Method

Heat the oil in a large pan and cook the onion, garlic and thyme for 5 minutes until softened. Stir in the rice, cook for a minute, then add the wine and boil vigorously for 2-3 minutes until the liquid has been absorbed. Pour in half the stock and simmer for 10 minutes or until the liquid has been absorbed, stirring from time to time.

Add the remaining stock, simmer for 5 minutes. Add the peas and beans, and cook, uncovered, for 5 minutes, stirring, until all the liquid has been absorbed and the rice is tender. Divide between bowls and top with the dolcelatte and black pepper.

Thai Crab & Coconut Rice (Serves 4)

175g/6oz white crab meat
1 tbsp groundnut or vegetable oil
1 tsp cumin seeds
1/2 tsp coriander seeds, crushed
1 large onion, thinly sliced
1/2 tsp turmeric
280g/10oz long-grain rice
200ml/7 fl oz half-fat coconut milk
1/2 tsp salt
3 tbsps chopped coriander

Method

Heat the oil in a medium pan, add the cumin and coriander seeds and toast for 1 minute over a medium heat. Add the onion and fry, stirring, for a further 5 minutes. Add the turmeric and rice and stir for 1 minute.

Pour in the coconut milk, then enough water to come 2.5cm/1inch above the surface of the rice. Stir in the salt and bring to the boil. Cover, reduce the heat to low and simmer gently for 10 minutes.

Remove from the heat and leave, covered, to steam for 10 minutes. Fluff up with a fork, fold in the crab and cover for a further minute, to heat through. Scatter over the coriander and serve.

Nasi Goreng (Serves 4)

300g/10 1/2oz long grain rice
3 tbsps light soy sauce
2 tsps light brown muscovado sugar
1 tbsp fish sauce
2 tbsps vegetable oil
1 red chilli, finely chopped
2 garlic cloves, crushed
200g/7oz king prawns
150g/5oz petits pois
8 spring onions, sliced
4 eggs

Method

Put the rice and 500ml/18 fl oz water into a pan. Bring to the boil, stir once, cover, then simmer for 10 minutes. Turn off the heat and leave the rice to steam for 10 minutes more.

Combine the soy sauce, sugar and fish sauce; set aside. When the rice is almost ready, heat half the oil a large frying pan or wok over a high heat. Add the chilli and garlic and fry for 1 minute. Add the prawns, fry for another minute, then add the peas and spring onions and cook for another couple of minutes, until the prawns are pink all over.

Toss the rice with the prawns and vegetables, then pour in the soy sauce mixture and stir-fry until evenly coated. Scoop into serving bowls. Wipe out the pan, return to a high heat and add the remaining oil. Fry the eggs for 3-4 minutes until the whites are set. Serve the fried eggs on top of the rice.

My recipes

Recipe --

Serves --

Preparation time --

Notes/tips --

Ingredients

-- --

-- --

-- --

-- --

-- --

-- --

Method

My recipes

Recipe --

Serves --

Preparation time --

Notes/tips --

Ingredients

-- --

-- --

-- --

-- --

-- --

-- --

-- --

Method

My recipes

Recipe ....

Serves ....

Preparation time ....

Notes/tips ....

....

....

....

Ingredients

....

....

....

....

....

....

....

Method

My recipes

Recipe ....

Serves ....

Preparation time ....

Notes/tips ....

....

....

....

Ingredients

....

....

....

....

....

....

....

....

Method

My recipes

Recipe ....

Serves ....

Preparation time ....

Notes/tips ....

....

....

....

Ingredients

....

....

....

....

....

....

....

....

Method

My recipes

Recipe _____

Serves _____

Preparation time _____

Notes/tips _____

_____

_____

_____

Ingredients

_____ _____

_____ _____

_____ _____

_____ _____

_____ _____

_____ _____

_____ _____

Method

My recipes

Recipe ....

Serves ....

Preparation time ....

Notes/tips ....

....

....

....

Ingredients

....

....

....

....

....

....

....

....

Method

_____

_____

_____

_____

_____

_____

_____

_____

_____

_____

_____

_____

_____

_____

My recipes

Recipe ....

Serves ....

Preparation time ....

Notes/tips ....

....

....

....

Ingredients

....

....

....

....

....

....

Method

vegetables & salads

Braised Red Cabbage with Apples

(Serves 6 generously)

A great accompaniment to cooked meat, hot or cold.

1.2kg/2lb red cabbage (finely shredded)
4 Granny Smiths apples (peeled, cored and roughly chopped)
300ml/10 1/2 fl oz cider
100g/3 1/2oz light brown soft sugar

Method

In a large saucepan arrange a layer of the cabbage in the bottom of the pan, add a layer of the apples and a sprinkling of the sugar, and season with salt and pepper. Continue to create layers until all the vegetables have been used up. Pour over the cider and add a good drizzle of olive oil. Bring to the boil, then simmer with a tight fitting lid, over a low heat for 1 and a half hours, until tender. The cabbage will keep for 2 days, covered in the fridge or in the freezer for up to 1 month. Reheat in either a pan or in the microwave.

Optional: Add 2 teaspoons of ground mixed spice and 3 tablespoons of cider vinegar to give the dish a little spice.

Glazed Carrots with Thyme (Serves 6)

1kg/2.2lb carrots (cut into chunky wedges)
2 tbsps golden caster sugar
4 sprigs thyme
50g/2oz butter
chopped parsley, optional

Method

Put the carrots, butter, sugar and thyme in a wide shallow pan with a lid, season with salt and pepper, then add water to come halfway up the carrots. Bring to a simmer, cover and cook until the carrots are almost tender (about 5-6 minutes). Turn up the heat, remove the lid and cook until all the liquid has evaporated and the carrots have taken on a beautiful glaze. Transfer to a warmed serving dish and garnish with freshly chopped parsley.

Crisp Honey & Mustard Parsnips (Serves 6)

1kg/2.2lb parsnips (peeled and cut into thumb-width batons)
2 tsps English mustard powder
2 tbsps plain flour
3 tsps clear honey

Method

Boil the parsnips for 2-3 minutes, drain well and let them steam dry for a few minutes. Mix the mustard powder with the flour and plenty of salt and freshly ground black pepper. Toss the parsnips in the mix, then shake off any excess. Heat oven to 220C/425F/Gas mark 7. In a large non-stick baking tray add 4 tablespoons of oil and place in the oven to heat for 5 minutes.

Carefully place the parsnips into the hot oil, ensuring all the parsnips are coated in the oil. Roast for 30 minutes or until golden and crisp. Drizzle the honey over the hot parsnips, give them a little shake, then scatter with flaky sea salt and serve in a warmed serving dish.

Potatoes Dauphinoise (Serves 4)

A delicious rich, hearty potato dish, an excellent accompaniment to steak.

1kg/2.2lb even-sized floury potatoes, such as King Edward or Maris Piper
1 onion, thinly sliced
280ml/10 fl oz double cream
75ml/2 1/2 fl oz milk

Method

Preheat oven to 190C/375F/Gas mark 5. Slice the potatoes as thinly as you can, either using a mandolin, or with a very sharp knife. Take a suitable sized baking dish and rub butter all over the base and the sides of the dish.

Layer up evenly with the onions and potatoes, seasoning with salt and freshly ground black pepper as you go. Pour over the cream and milk, dot pieces of butter over the top. Cover with foil.

Place on a baking sheet and bake for 1 hour. Discard the foil and bake for a further 10-15 minutes or until the potatoes are cooked through and golden brown on top.

Cheesy Broccoli Bake (Serves 6 generously)

450g/1lb broccoli florets
8 spring onions, finely chopped
200g/7oz cherry tomatoes, halved or quartered
2 large eggs, beaten
200g/7oz cottage cheese
3 garlic cloves, peeled and crushed
salt and freshly ground black pepper
4 tbsps finely chopped parsley
110g/4oz cheddar cheese, grated

Method

Preheat the oven to 220C/425F/Gas mark 7. Cook the broccoli in a large saucepan of lightly salted boiling water for 2-3 minutes. Drain, transfer to a bowl and set aside. Add the spring onions and cherry tomatoes to the broccoli, mix well and spoon into an ovenproof dish.

Meanwhile, whisk the eggs in a clean bowl with the cottage cheese and garlic until smooth. Season well and add the parsley then pour the egg mixture over the vegetables and stir briefly to distribute the ingredients evenly. Sprinkle the cheddar cheese on top and cook in the oven for 15-20 minutes or until the mixture has just set.

Layered Roast Summer Vegetables

(Serves 4)

This all in one side dish can double up as a vegetarian main course.

4 large courgettes (thickly sliced)
5 ripe plum tomatoes, sliced
2 aubergines, sliced
1 large garlic bulb

Method

Heat the oven to 220C/425F/Gas mark 7. Drizzle a round ovenproof dish with a little olive oil, then, starting from the outside, tightly layer alternate slices of the vegetables in concentric circles until you get to the middle.

Sit the head of garlic in the middle. If you have any vegetables left, tuck them into the gaps around the outside. Drizzle everything generously with olive oil then season with salt and freshly ground black pepper.

Roast, drizzling with more oil occasionally, for 50 minutes to 1 hour, until the vegetables are soft and lightly charred. Remove from the oven and leave to stand for a few minutes, then remove the garlic and separate into cloves for squeezing over the vegetables.

Optional: Place sprigs of rosemary or thyme between the layers of vegetables during cooking. Also try crumbling feta cheese on top of the vegetables for the last 10 minutes cooking time, delicious.

Thai Satay Vegetable Stir Fry (Serves 4)

3 tbsps crunchy peanut butter
3 tbsps sweet chilli sauce
2 tbsps soy sauce
1 tbsp oil
small piece of ginger, peeled and grated
300g/10 1/2oz ready to wok noodles
300g/10 1/2oz stir fry pack of vegetables
25g/1oz dry roasted peanuts
1 tbsp torn basil leaves
100ml/3 1/2 fl oz water

Method

Mix the peanut butter with the chilli sauce, 100ml/3 1/2 fl oz water and the soy sauce to make the satay sauce. Heat the oil in a wok, stir fry the vegetables for 2 minutes, add the noodles and ginger then cook over a high heat for 2 minutes. Push the vegetables and noodles to one side in the pan and add the sauce, bring to the boil. Mix all the veg and noodles until thoroughly combined with the sauce. Sprinkle over the torn basil leaves and peanuts and serve.

Pear, Blue Cheese & Walnut Salad

(Serves 4)

2 under ripe pears (peeled, cored and thinly sliced lengthways)
110g/4oz blue cheese, roughly cubed
selection of salad leaves (rocket or radicchio are particulary good here)
handful of walnut pieces
2 tsps honey
85ml/3 fl oz extra-virgin olive oil
1 tbsp white wine vinegar

Method

Mix together the honey, oil and vinegar to create a dressing. Remove the cores from the pears and slice thinly, leaving skin on. Place in a bowl and pour over the dressing.

Combine the salad leaves, blue cheese and walnuts on a serving platter. Scatter with the pears, drizzle over the dressing and serve.

Simple Potato Salad (Serves 6)

Great for summer barbecues and picnics, quick and easy to make and goes well with grilled meats and fish.

1kg/2.2lb new potatoes, scrubbed
1 small red onion, finely sliced
2 tbsps capers, rinsed and drained
6 tbsps extra virgin olive oil
juice of half a lemon

Method

Place the potatoes in boiling salted water and simmer for 10-12 minutes until just tender. Drain well and tip into a serving bowl. In a separate bowl, mix together the onion, olive oil, capers and the juice of half a lemon.

Season to taste with salt and freshly ground black pepper. Pour over the warmed potatoes and serve, garnished with a large handful of freshly chopped parsley leaves.

Optional: Try one of these delicious variations.

Spiced Yoghurt & Mint:
Mix 200ml/7 fl oz natural yoghurt, juice of half a lemon, 1 teaspoon of ground cumin and a handful of chopped fresh mint. Add to the cooked, cooled potatoes and stir and coat.

Sun Dried Tomato & Basil:
Mix 6 tablespoons extra virgin olive oil, 2 tablespoons balsamic vinegar, a handful of torn basil leaves, and 100g/3 1/2 oz sun dried tomatoes. Toss to coat in the warmed potatoes. Season to taste with salt and pepper.

Walnut, Orange & Tarragon:
Mix 6 tablespoons of walnut oil, the zest and juice of half an orange, a handful of chopped fresh tarragon and 100g/3 1/2 oz of chopped walnuts. Toss to coat in the warm potatoes.

Grape & Halloumi Salad

(Serves 2)

150g/5oz mixed salad leaves
50g/2oz mixed fresh herbs
175g/6oz mixed seedless grapes
250g/9oz halloumi cheese
75ml/2 1/2 fl oz vinaigrette
2 tbsps olive oil
squeeze of lemon juice

Method

Mix together the salad leaves, the fresh herbs and the mixed grapes in a large serving bowl. Make a simple dressing by mixing the vinaigrette, oil and lemon juice.

Slice the halloumi cheese thinly and place in a large non-stick pan over a medium heat. Cook until the underside starts to turn a golden brown then flip to cook the other side.

Place the warm cheese on top of the salad leaves and drizzle with the dressing. Serve while the cheese is still hot.

Warm Pea & Lentil Salad (Serves 4)

This warm pea and lentil salad has an exciting sharp contrast between flavours and textures – nutty lentils with fresh green peas. This light tasting vegetable dish works well as a light lunch or starter.

200g/7oz puy lentils
200g/7oz fresh or frozen peas
4 tbsps olive oil
2 garlic cloves, peeled
salt and black pepper
juice of 2 limes

Method

Wash, rinse and drain the lentils, cook in unsalted water with the garlic for about 20 minutes, until they are tender but still with some bite. Drain and place in a large warmed serving bowl. Remove the garlic and squash to a paste.

Add 4 tablespoons of good olive oil, the lime juice, garlic paste and a generous seasoning of salt and freshly ground black pepper. Meanwhile blanch the peas in boiling salted water for no more than 1-2 minutes, drain and add to the lentils. Mix all the ingredients together until thoroughly combined, and serve with warm crusty bread.

Caesar Salad (Serves 4)

2 Romaine lettuce hearts, rinsed and dried
110g/4oz parmesan, coarsely grated
50g/2oz of anchovy fillets
For the croutons
3 tbsps extra virgin olive oil
1 small white baguette, cubed
1 large clove garlic, crushed
For the dressing
salt and freshly ground black pepper
75ml/2 1/2 fl oz extra virgin olive oil
2 tbsps lemon juice
1 tsp Worcestershire sauce
1 clove garlic, finely chopped
1 tsp Dijon mustard
1 tbsp mayonnaise

Method

Preheat the oven to 190C/375F/Gas mark 5. To make the croutons, toss the bread in a mixture of the olive oil and crushed garlic and spread over a baking sheet. Cook for 15-20 minutes until golden and crisp. Leave to cool.

Using your hands, tear the lettuce into bite-sized pieces and place in a salad bowl then make the dressing by whisking the lemon juice and Worcestershire sauce together with the garlic, mustard and seasoning.

Whisk in the mayonnaise, then gradually whisk in the oil until the dressing is thick and creamy. Add the dressing to the lettuce and toss. Add the parmesan, anchovies and croutons and toss lightly. Serve immediately. If you wish you can add warm, sliced chicken breast fillets to the salad to make a more substantial meal.

Rocket & Mozzarella Salad (Serves 4)

150g/5oz rocket leaves
250g/9oz buffalo mozzarella pearls (or buffalo mozzarella, sliced)
8 plum or vine ripened tomatoes, quartered or sliced
1 garlic clove crushed
handful of basil leaves shredded
sea salt and freshly ground pepper
2 tbsps extra virgin olive oil
2 tsps balsamic vinegar

Method

Place the tomatoes in a bowl, add the garlic and a little salt and pepper. Toss and leave it to stand for about 5 minutes to infuse. Add the rocket leaves to the tomatoes then add the mozzarella, and basil leaves. Dish the salad out on to four plates. Drizzle the olive oil and balsamic vinegar around the plate to serve.

Haddock, Potato & Smoked Bacon Salad with Poached Egg (Serves 6)

400g/14oz smoked haddock fillets
450g/1lb salad or new potatoes scrubbed
200g/7oz smoked bacon lardons
handful of fresh parsley, finely chopped
freshly ground black pepper
200g/7oz rocket

For the poached eggs
6 eggs
2 tsps white wine vinegar

For the dressing
1 tbsp lemon juice
2 tsps wholegrain mustard
salt and freshly ground black pepper
3 tbsps olive oil
4 tbsps soured cream

Method

Slice the potatoes and cook in a pan of boiling water for 8-10 minutes, until tender. Drain and cool then cook the lardons gently in a frying pan without any extra fat, until the fat starts to melt, then increase the heat and fry them until they are crisp and browned.

Remove and drain them on kitchen paper. To cook the fish, cut the fillets to fit the frying pan. Place in the pan and cover with a pint each of milk and water.

Simmer gently for 2-3 minutes each side (depending on thickness of fillets). Remove from the liquid with a slotted spoon. Cool the fish slightly, then peel off and discard the skin and break the flesh into large flakes.

Whisk the dressing ingredients with a fork until smooth. Meanwhile, fill a large saucepan with water 10cm/4inches deep, add the vinegar, and bring to a simmer. Break the eggs and slip into the water. Poach for 3-4 minutes. Remove with a slotted spoon.

To make the salad, divide the potatoes between six side plates, then top with the haddock and drizzle with dressing. Sprinkle with the lardons then top with the soft poached egg and finish with and black pepper.

Greek Salad (Serves 4)

350g/12 oz vine rippened tomatoes
1 medium cucumber, peeled and finely sliced into rounds
1 red onion, halved and finely sliced
salt and freshly ground black pepper
3-4 tbsps extra virgin olive oil
200g/7oz Feta cheese
pinch of dried oregano
12 black olives

Method

Quarter the tomatoes. Mix the tomato wedges with the cucumber and onion then season very lightly before gently tossing in olive oil to taste. Divide the salad between four serving bowls, and add the Feta, arranging all the ingredients carefully.

Season with some dried oregano and add the black olives. Finally, drizzle a little more olive oil over the salad and serve straight away, as a starter or side dish.

My recipes

Recipe ....

Serves ....

Preparation time ....

Notes/tips

....

....

....

Ingredients

....

....

....

....

....

....

....

Method

My recipes

Recipe --

Serves --

Preparation time --

Notes/tips --

Ingredients

------------------------------- -------------------------------

------------------------------- -------------------------------

------------------------------- -------------------------------

------------------------------- -------------------------------

------------------------------- -------------------------------

------------------------------- -------------------------------

------------------------------- -------------------------------

Method

My recipes

Recipe ---

Serves ---

Preparation time ---

Notes/tips ---

Ingredients ---

Method

My recipes

Recipe ....

Serves ....

Preparation time ....

Notes/tips ....

....

....

....

Ingredients ....

....

....

....

....

....

....

Method

My recipes

Recipe ....

Serves ....

Preparation time ....

Notes/tips ....

....

....

....

Ingredients

....

....

....

....

....

....

....

....

Method

My recipes

Recipe --

Serves --

Preparation time --

Notes/tips --

Ingredients --

-- --

-- --

-- --

-- --

-- --

-- --

-- --

-- --

Method

My recipes

Recipe --

Serves --

Preparation time ------------------------------------

Notes/tips --

Ingredients

------------------------------------   ------------------------------------

------------------------------------   ------------------------------------

------------------------------------   ------------------------------------

------------------------------------   ------------------------------------

------------------------------------   ------------------------------------

------------------------------------   ------------------------------------

------------------------------------   ------------------------------------

------------------------------------   ------------------------------------

Method

sweet treats

Lime Cheesecake with Chocolate Chip Biscuit Base (Serves 8)

50g/2oz unsalted butter, cut into chunks
150g/5oz pack chocolate chip cookies,
1 x 135g pack lime flavoured jelly
200ml/7 fl oz evaporated milk, chilled
200g/7 oz pack soft cheese
3 limes

Method

Line the base of a 20cm x 5cm(8 x 2inch) round loose-bottomed sandwich tin with baking parchment. Crush the cookies into small pieces - the easiest way to do this is to put them in a plastic bag, tie the bag closed and then bash with a rolling pin. Melt the butter in a saucepan and stir in the crushed biscuits. Press the mixture into the base of the prepared sandwich tin and chill for at least an hour.

In a bowl, dissolve the jelly in 100ml/3 1/2 fl oz boiling water. Stir with a spoon then set aside to cool. Meanwhile, whisk the evaporated milk until light and fluffy, and has doubled in volume. Then whisk in the cream cheese until smooth and well combined.

Take the finely grated zest and juice of 2 of the limes. Slice the remaining lime and set aside. Add all the juice and half of the zest to the cream cheese mix then whisk in the jelly. Pour over the biscuit base and chill for 2 hours or until set. Decorate with the reserved lime zest and slices of lime.

Sherry Trifle (Serves 6-8)

An old favourite, this recipe uses home made custard which is deliciously smooth and creamy, combined with sweet jelly, sherry infused sponge and soft summer fruits which make this trifle so delicious.

1 x 135g packet, raspberry or strawberry jelly
175g/6oz sponge fingers
5 tbsps sherry
150g/5oz raspberries
150g/5oz strawberries, hulled and halved

For the custard
300ml/10 1/2 fl oz milk
300ml/10 1/2 fl oz double cream
1 vanilla pod, split, seeds scraped out
2 tbsps cornflour
4 large eggs
75g/2 1/2oz caster sugar

For the topping
25g/1oz toasted flaked almonds
300ml/10 1/2 fl oz double cream, lightly whipped

Method

Prepare the jelly as per instruction on the packet. Break the sponge fingers into the base of a large serving bowl. Pour the sherry over the fingers and allow to soak in. Scatter the fruit over the soaked sponge, then pour the jelly over the top of the sponge and fruit. Chill in the fridge for 2 hours or until the jelly has set.

Meanwhile to make the custard, pour the milk and cream into a heavy based saucepan, add the vanilla pod and seeds then slowly bring to the boil. Once the mixture has come to the boil, remove from the heat and leave to infuse for 10 minutes. Remove the vanilla pod.

Mix the cornflour with 2 tablespoons of water until smooth. Whisk the egg yolks with the sugar in a large bowl until well combined. Gradually add the warmed milk and cream into the egg yolks, whisking until smooth.

Return the mixture to the saucepan, add the cornflour mixture and cook over a low heat stirring continuously for about 6-8 minutes until the custard has thickened enough to coat the back of a wooden spoon. Do not allow the custard to boil, this will cause the mixture to curdle. Remove the custard from the heat, then strain through a sieve into a bowl set over a bowl of iced water to cool the mixture. Cover the surface of the custard with cling film to prevent a skin forming.

When the custard is cool give it a really good stir until it is very smooth, then pour over the set jelly. Return to the fridge for 30 minutes until the custard is lightly set. Remove from the fridge and spoon over the lightly whipped cream and top with the toasted flaked almonds. Return the trifle to the fridge until ready to serve.

Pavlova (Serves 8)

300g/10 1/2oz mixed summer berries
6 egg whites
200g/7oz caster sugar
280ml/10 fl oz double cream
1 tsp cornflour
1 tsp vinegar

Method

Preheat the oven to 170C/325F/Gas mark 3 and line a baking tray with non stick baking paper. Whisk the egg whites with an electric whisk on high speed and gradually add the caster sugar, reduce the speed, add the cornflour and vinegar, return to a high speed and mix until the meringue is stiff and glossy.

Spread the meringue with a spatula into a circle onto the lined baking sheet and place in the oven. Turn off the oven and leave for 4-6 hours or overnight to dry out. Lightly whip 280ml/10 fl oz of double cream to form soft peaks, spread onto the cooled pavlova, top with a the mixed berries.

Black Cherry Ice Cream (Serves 6)

You don't need an ice-cream machine to make this rich and creamy treat.

3 egg yolks
75g/2 1/2oz granulated sugar
250ml/9 fl oz whipping cream
2 tsps vanilla essence
For the cherries
450g/1lb chopped pitted sweet black cherries
130g/4 1/2 oz granulated sugar

Method

In a bowl, whisk together the egg yolks with the sugar for 2 minutes or until it is pale and thickened, then set aside. In a heavy saucepan, heat the cream and over medium-high heat just until bubbles form around edge; gradually whisk into yolk mixture.

Return to saucepan then cook over a low heat, stirring constantly, for about 12 minutes or until thick enough to coat back of wooden spoon. Immediately strain through a fine sieve into large bowl. Stir in the vanilla essence then refrigerate for about 2 hours or until chilled or for up to 24 hours.

Meanwhile, in a bowl, combine the cherries with sugar and let stand for about 2 hours. Stir into the chilled cream mixture.

Pour into a shallow metal dish, cover, then freeze for at least 3 hours or until almost firm. Break up into chunks then transfer to a food processor and process until smooth. Transfer to a chilled airtight container and freeze for a minimum of 1 hour or until firm.

Chocolate Mousse

(Serves 6)

250g/9oz plain chocolate, chopped
130ml/4 1/2 fl oz water
25g/1oz butter
3 egg yolks
2 tbsps sugar
300ml/10 1/2 fl oz whipping cream,
whipped

Method

A Bain Marie (or water bath) is a piece
of equipment used to heat ingredients
gently and gradually. You can use a
microwave, as an alternative.

Heat the chocolate, 60ml water and
butter in the Bain Marie until the
chocolate and butter are melted.

Remove from the heat and cool for 10
minutes. In a small heavy saucepan,
whisk egg yolks, sugar and remaining
water. Cook and stir over low heat until
mixture reaches 70 degrees C, about
1-2 minutes.

Remove from the heat and whisk in the
chocolate mixture. Set the saucepan in
ice and stir until cooled, about 5-10
minutes. Fold in the whipped cream.
Spoon into six dessert glasses.
Refrigerate for 4 hours or overnight.
Serve with additional whipped cream on
top if you like.

158

Tiramisu (Serves 6)

Classic Italian dessert, rich, boozy, smooth and silky, a delicious end to any meal.

250g/9oz mascarpone
1 tsp vanilla extract
50g/2oz caster sugar
3 egg yolks
250ml/9 fl oz double cream, very lightly whipped
4 tbsps brandy or rum
about 300g/10 1/2oz sponge fingers
350ml/12 fl oz strong black coffee
2-3 tbsps cocoa powder

Method

In a heatproof bowl set over a pan of gently simmering water, whisk together the eggs yolks and caster sugar with the vanilla extract, until thick and creamy. The mixture is ready when a trail forms when you lift up the whisk. Remove from the heat and leave to cool.

When cool, beat in the mascarpone, then gently fold in the whipped cream. Mix the coffee with the brandy or rum in a small shallow dish, then dip the Italian sponge fingers into the coffee, making sure they are completely immersed. (Do not leave them in for to long as they will break up, but make sure they are well soaked). Arrange the soaked biscuits in the base of a large serving dish or individual dishes or coffee cups.

Cover the fingers with some of the creamy mascarpone mixture, then repeat the process, building up in layers until all the mix is used up, finishing with the cream mixture. Sift the cocoa powder on top in an even layer. Cover and chill in the fridge for 2 hours before serving.

My recipes

Recipe ---

Serves ---

Preparation time ---

Notes/tips ---

Ingredients

--------------------------------- ---------------------------------

--------------------------------- ---------------------------------

--------------------------------- ---------------------------------

--------------------------------- ---------------------------------

--------------------------------- ---------------------------------

--------------------------------- ---------------------------------

--------------------------------- ---------------------------------

Method

My recipes

Recipe ....

Serves ....

Preparation time ....

Notes/tips ....

....

....

....

Ingredients

....

....

....

....

....

....

....

....

Method

My recipes

Recipe ....

Serves ....

Preparation time ....

Notes/tips ....

....

....

....

Ingredients

....

....

....

....

....

....

....

....

Method

My recipes

Recipe --

Serves --

Preparation time --

Notes/tips --

Ingredients

-- --

-- --

-- --

-- --

-- --

-- --

-- --

Method

My recipes

Recipe ....

Serves ....

Preparation time ....

Notes/tips ....

....

....

....

Ingredients

....

....

....

....

....

....

....

....

....

....

....

....

Method

My recipes

Recipe --

Serves --

Preparation time --

Notes/tips --

Ingredients

-- --

-- --

-- --

-- --

-- --

-- --

-- --

Method

My recipes

Recipe ....

Serves ....

Preparation time ....

Notes/tips ....

....

....

....

Ingredients

....

....

....

....

....

....

....

Method

List of recipes

Spanish Style Chicken, 73
Duck Pancakes & Hoisin Sauce, 74
Partridge with Mushroom Bruschettas, 75

Pasta & rice
Pasta Carbonara, 92
Spaghetti with Chilli, Olive Oil & Garlic, 93
Ragu Sauce, 93
Pappardelle alla Bolognese, 95
Lasagne, 96
Wild Mushrooms Risotto, 97
Garden Pea & Broad Bean Risotto with Dolcelatte, 98
Thai Crab & Coconut Rice, 99
Nasi Goreng, 101

Vegetables & salads
Braised Red Cabbage with Apples, 120
Glazed Carrots with Thyme, 121
Crisp Honey & Mustard Parsnips, 121
Potatoes Dauphinoise, 123
Cheesy Broccoli Bake, 123
Layered Roast Summer Vegetables, 125
Thai Satay Vegetable Stir Fry, 126
Pear, Blue Cheese & Walnut Salad, 127
Simple Potato Salad, 128
Grape & Halloumi Salad, 129
Warm Pea & Lentil Salad, 130
Caesar Salad, 131
Rocket & Mozzarella Salad, 132
Haddock, Potato & Smoked Bacon Salad with Poached Egg, 133
Greek Salad, 134

Sweet treats
Lime Cheesecake with Chocolate Chip Biscuit Base, 152
Sherry Trifle, 153
Pavlova, 154
Black Cherry Ice Cream, 157
Chocolate Mousse, 158
Tiramisu, 159

Spoons to millilitres

1/2 teaspoon	2.5 ml	1 tablespoon	15 ml
1 teaspoon	5 ml	2 tablespoons	30 ml
1 & 1/2 teaspoons	7.5 ml	3 tablespoons	45 ml
2 teaspoons	10 ml	4 tablespoons	60 ml

Grams to ounces

10g	0.25oz	225g	8oz
15g	0.38oz	250g	9oz
25g	1oz	280g	10oz
50g	2oz	325g	11oz
85g	3oz	350g	12oz
110g	4oz	375g	13oz
150g	5oz	400g	14oz
175g	6oz	425g	15oz
200g	7oz	450g	16oz/1lb

Liquid measures

5fl oz	1/4 pint	150 ml	
7.5fl oz		215 ml	
10fl oz	1/2 pint	280 ml	
15fl oz		425 ml	
20fl oz	1 pint	570 ml	
35fl oz		1 litre	

The recipes contained in this book are passed on in good faith but the publisher cannot be held responsible for any adverse results. Please be aware that certain recipes may contain nuts. Spoon measurements are level, teaspoons are assumed to be 5ml, tablespoons 15ml. For other measurements, see chart above. Times given are for guidance only, as preparation techniques may vary and can lead to different cooking times.